Mom —

As I read through this book, so many of these statements reminded me of you. Happy Birthday and may you enjoy many more. I love you!

Teri

A Gift For:

From:

Published by Hallmark Gift Books,
a division of Hallmark Cards, Inc.,
Kansas City, MO 64141
Visit us on the Web at Hallmark.com.

Editorial Director: Delia Berrigan
Editor: Kara Goodier
Art Director: Chris Opheim
Designer: Laura Elsenraat
Production Designer: Dan Horton

ISBN: 978-1-63059-994-2
BOK2251

Made in China

UNIQUELY
MOM

A MIGHTY, AMAZING, EXTRAORDINARY WOMAN

Hallmark

A really extraordinary mom

has the gift of making others

feel at home in her family.

MOM

puts the heart in home.

A MOM DOES ONE OF THE WORLD'S TOUGHEST JOBS...

AND MAKES IT LOOK EASY.

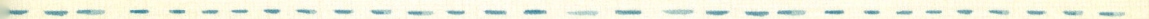

There's no such thing
as an ordinary mom.

MORE THAN HERSELF, LONGER THAN FOREVER—

THAT'S HOW A MOTHER LOVES.

HOW MOMS DO IT:

Patience. A sense of humor.
Deep breaths. Caffeine. Plenty of heart.
All the help they can get.

The perfect balance between kisses and hugs
and the occasional kick in the pants.

Being a mom is a BIG JOB

made up of a bazillion little jobs.

Being a mom
takes an exceptional
kind of love.

That takes an exceptional kind of woman.

STEADY, FAITHFUL,

ENDLESS...

A MOM'S LOVE.

LAUNDRY, TOO.

But mostly her love.

You cannot judge a

MOM

until you've walked a mile
in her old slippers
that she refuses to replace
until everyone else
has everything they need.

Now these three remain:

FAITH, HOPE, & LOVE.

And the greatest combination of all three is

MOM.

Just what you need,
just when you need it—
that's mom-love.

24/7
TENDERNESS
AND TOUGHNESS.

A MOM CAN DO FIVE THINGS AT ONCE.

(EIGHT, IF SHE'S HAD AN EXTRA TEN MINUTES OF SLEEP.)

Moms don't do it for the thanks or praise.

They care for us, listen to us, believe in us...

just because they love us.

A mom stops at nothing
to give you everything.

THERE'S NO PLACE LIKE MOM'S...
for delicious food,
for amazing hugs,
for sheets that smell like sunshine,
for taking it easy,
for heart-to-heart talks,

AND FOR FEELING LOVED.

What does it take to be a mom?

EVERYTHING. And then some.

HOW TO HELP.

HOW TO HEAL.

HOW TO LISTEN.

HOW TO LOVE.

There aren't rules for those things...
moms somehow just know.

Moms

teach us all the important stuff.
Almost any food can be turned into a casserole;
some items, like toothbrushes, should NOT be shared;
most emergency room surgeons
double as underwear inspectors; you'll need
the jacket later; ice cream always makes it better.

So many days,
it's a mom's wisdom
that makes
all the difference.

MOM

Little word. Big love.

Being a mom is the most heartwarming, exhausting, demanding, amazing, outrageously hopeful experience on earth...

and she does it beautifully.

She teaches us
what is worth celebrating,
worth nurturing,
worth honoring.

There's no one like a mom
to set you straight
and tend to your heart,
all at the same time.

A MOM'S LOVE IS AS STRONG AS A HURRICANE
AND AS SOFT AS A WHISPER.

UNLESS YOU MAKE HER MAD.

THEN IT'S KINDA LOUD.

Sweet, caring, good-hearted.
But also not to be messed with.

In Mom's house...
there is togetherness.
There is staying up too late talking.
There is laughing yourself silly.
There are good memories.

LOVE ON THE GO.

AND OFF THE GO.

ALWAYS, REALLY.

A mom
will let you laugh
until you cry
and cry
until you laugh.

"M-O-M"
spells love and warmth,
softness and strength,
laughter and friendship.

"M-O-M"

spells beautiful things.

TO BE A MOM
IS TO DO THE BEST YOU CAN
WITH WHAT YOU'VE GOT.

ABOUT A THOUSAND
TIMES A DAY.

ENCOURAGE, SUPPORT, SACRIFICE, INSPIRE…

Love isn't a big enough word to describe what moms do.

All the things
that make a good mom—
KINDNESS, THOUGHTFULNESS,
PATIENCE, STRENGTH, AND BEAUTY—

make an incredible woman.

MOMS AND SUNSHINE?
Basically the same thing.

IT'S SCIENCE.

MOMS KNOW WHEN TO LET YOU
SPREAD YOUR WINGS AND FLY...

AND WHEN TO PACK AN EXTRA PARACHUTE,

just in case.

MOM PUTS THE "HER" IN "HERO."

A mom can make an adventure
out of a trip to the grocery store,
a rainbow out of a cloudy-day mood.

Mom can turn any day into a
"going to remember this forever" day.

A mom is the friend
we all need in this crazy,
beautiful world.

Good listener?
CHECK.
Quick to laugh?
UH-HUH.
There for everything?
YEP.
Up for anything?
YOU BET.

MOM
IS EVERYTHING
AMAZING.

A mom can take the place of all others...

but no one else can take her place.

Only a mom understands just how hard, hilarious,
life-changing, crazy-making, messy, joyous...

humbling, creative, and downright
AMAZING being a mom really is.

She has a way
of listening to troubles
and making them
fade away.

Moms don't have to understand, do you favors,
laugh with you, hold your hand, see you through...

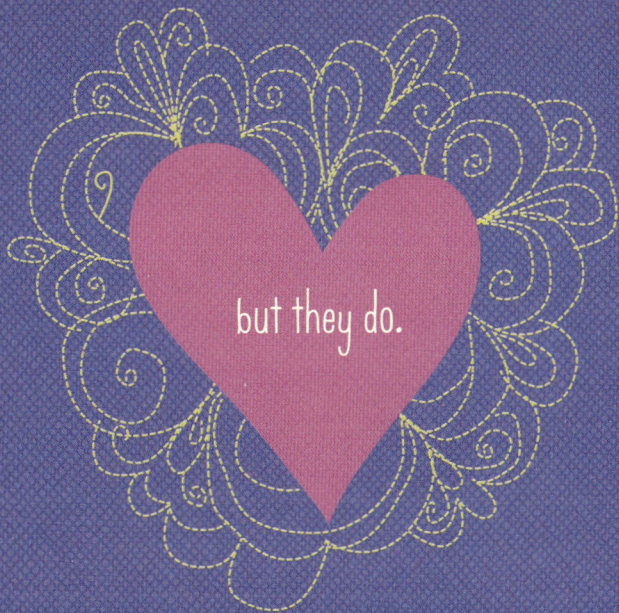

but they do.

Mom

is a map to life and love,

an emotional support and confidante,

a beautiful example of giving,

understanding, compassion, and kindness.

Mom makes
all the difference.

IF YOU HAVE ENJOYED THIS BOOK
OR IT HAS TOUCHED YOUR LIFE IN SOME WAY,
WE WOULD LOVE TO HEAR FROM YOU.

Please send comments to:
Hallmark Book Feedback
P.O. Box 419034
Mail Drop 215
Kansas City, MO 64141
Or email us at:
booknotes@hallmark.com